MY
MIND
BOOK

"An excellent introduction and resource for children to learn positive coping tools. It offers practical strategies for parents to help support their children, and is a gentle reminder for adults to disengage from egoic thought. The final five tips are especially useful!" — Ciara Williams-Gossen, Mother and Children's Yoga Instructor

"Children have a natural desire and gift for love. Unfortunately, frightening life experiences can forge negative thoughts into engrained beliefs. Fiona Williams has written a simple yet eloquent guide for children to reinspire their natural gifts for love." — Dr. Tim Hall, D.S.W., R.S.W., M.P.A, Former VP of Alberta Children's Hospital

"*My Mind Book* is a practical guide for kids on how to be their best and most true self. Its powerful and simply stated principles are easy to grasp, and focus on teaching awareness and presence in everyday situations. It not only will help children embrace the natural essence of love and kindness within their own hearts, but will potentially empower the same practice in family, friends and anyone they meet along life's path." — Jennifer Williams, ATP™, Reiki Master, and ACIM Practitioner

"*My Mind Book* takes a child through the concept of concrete laws, such as gravity and stopping at a stop sign, to lead them to understanding more subtle and yet just as real laws of how the mind affects one's life. Using captivating illustrations and brilliant explanations, she unfolds for children the concepts of cause and effect and the range of possible ways of thinking. Ultimately this book teaches children that they are very powerful sculptors of their own lives." — Lois Freisleben-Cook, MD, FAAP, Developmental Pediatrician in Arcata, CA.

"Teaching children how their minds work seems so important. Yet this is rarely taught! *My Mind Book* fills this need by teaching children simple yet powerful laws of mind — that positive thinking makes us feel happy, that forgiveness heals the mind, that we gain by giving, and that we are all connected." — Corinne Zupko, Ed.S., M.A., B.C.C., author and founder of FromAnxietyToLove.com

"This book is an encyclopedia on how to feel good!! Fiona Williams answers the question that was left unanswered for a century or more, 'Why do I not feel good and what can I do to stop this feeling?' And she answers it right. You can't NOT buy this book for your children, it will help them and you!" — Joaquin Gossen, Age 9

My Mind Book

CALL TO MIND BOOKS

CALGARY • CANADA

MY MIND BOOK

by Fiona Maria Williams

Illustrated by David Wiliams

CALL TO MIND BOOKS
www.fionamaria.ca

ISBN: 978-0-9950415-0-9

Designed and Produced by the
Fearless Assisted Publishing Program
www.fearlessbooks.com

Table of Contents

Dedication

This book is dedicated to all the children in the world.
From every corner, every race, and every faith or from no faith,
this is for you. You are all equal. May you learn and understand
how your minds work so you can achieve all your goals,
happily learn from the lessons presented to you,
and enjoy your life. May you also know how
welcome you are in this world.

Remember this always:
"You are wholly loving and wholly lovable."
— A COURSE IN MIRACLES

There are many laws which exist!

There are laws that rule our universe,
like the law of gravity.

Gravity keeps our feet planted on the ground
so we don't float up into space.

1

There are laws that keep us safe,

like stopping at a **STOP** sign.

But did you know
that there are
laws for
your
MIND?

That's right!

There are
laws
for your
thinking!

3

The laws of the mind are here to
help you!

To help you understand your thoughts
and your feelings, and to help you
understand others.

Since ALL of your thoughts and ALL of your ideas
come from your mind,
then
it makes
sense to
understand
HOW your
mind works,
right?

Cool!
Let's get
started!

Cause and Effect

Cause is the start of something.

In our world, everything starts
with a thought or an idea
in your mind.

Effect is what you feel
after you think.

Are you
happy?

Angry?

Afraid?

Or
maybe
you
feel the
fluttering
of butterflies
in your
stomach...

All these feelings
are effects.

5

Your Thoughts Can Be Fearful or Loving

One thought cannot be both fearful and loving; a thought is either one or the other.

Fearful thoughts cause you to feel angry, scared, or even sad. These thoughts hurt your mind.

Loving thoughts are good! They make you feel **EXCITED, HAPPY,** or *peaceful*.

These are the types of thoughts that make you smile.

6

Your Mind Can Only Think One Thought at a Time

Does it sometimes feel like your mind is *RACING*?

Or like there is a parade of thoughts marching through your head?

7

Sometimes it may be hard to fall asleep.

Sometimes you may feel unfocused at school because there are so many thoughts passing through your mind.

But, you can choose to slow down your thinking.

R e l a x, take some deep breaths and choose to focus on one loving thought at a time. This will calm your mind down.

8

Your Thoughts Grow Stronger the More You Share them

Let's say that you are scared of something and you choose to share what you are afraid of with all of your friends and anyone else who will listen. By sharing this thought so many times, you have made the scary idea stronger in your own mind!

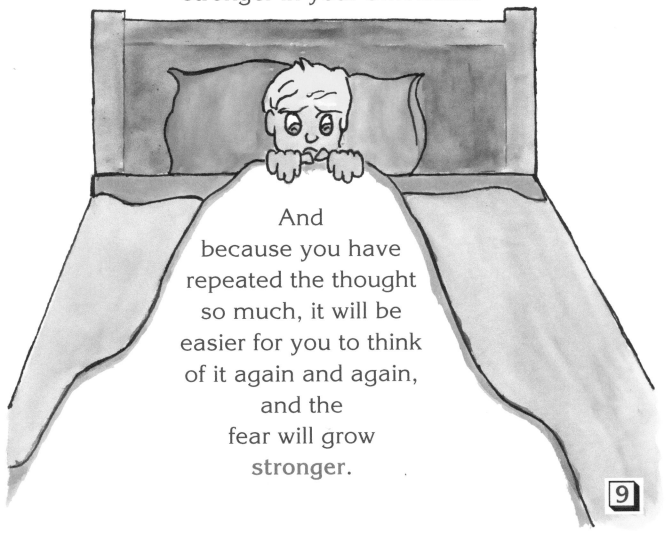

And because you have repeated the thought so much, it will be easier for you to think of it again and again, and the fear will grow stronger.

9

If you need help moving past a scary thought, then go talk to someone you trust.

You are not alone and there are so many people who care about you!

It is *always* safe for you to ask for help.

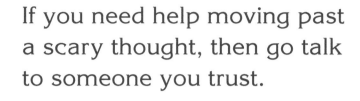

Speaking to one person you trust when you are afraid or worried is a good thing! That person can help you think lovingly.

And what if you were to share loving thoughts? You will smile more, and everyone will smile with you.

So, if you want to share a loving thought with everyone, go for it!

All Minds Are Connected

Just
because you
don't see your thoughts,
it doesn't mean they
cannot be shared.

They are just like music travelling through radio waves, or even the warmth of a campfire moving through heatwaves. You don't see these waves of music or heat, but you know they are there.

You hear the music
and you feel the heat
from the campfire.

Thoughts are
the same.

We are all tuning into each other's thoughts all the time.

Sometimes you may experience this when you and a friend say the same thing at the same time.

And so, we help ourselves and each other by thinking lovingly.

Never underestimate the **POWER** of a **POSITIVE** thought!

What You Think About Others Is What You Actually Think About Yourself

When you call someone a name or
say something mean to another person,
you are actually saying it to
yourself!

13

When you
see the
BEST
in others,
you see the
BEST
in yourself!

This is
a <u>GOOD</u> habit
to start!

By seeing the
BEST in others
you will
BOOST
your self-esteem
and you will
feel
happier
more often!

Your Thoughts Turn Into Your Beliefs

You have already learned that when you share and repeat thoughts, they will grow **STRONGER.**

A belief is an idea that you feel strongly about.

This idea became a belief because you repeated it so much.

Sometimes you may even find yourself standing up for your beliefs!

15

If you believe in something negative about yourself, then you are hurting yourself.

Here is a helpful idea: You can change negative thoughts about yourself by doing "The Switch"!

"The Switch" is when you switch a negative thought to a positive thought.

Practice "The Switch" whenever you are feeling negative about yourself.

16

Your Actions Come From How You Think

When you believe in your thoughts, you may choose to act on them.

If you are feeling angry or upset and you choose to act from those negative thoughts, you may end up doing or saying something hurtful.

When you act on positive thoughts, you will be *Loving*. Then your actions will be patient and kind.

Always ask yourself if what you are about to do is *Loving* for everyone.

17

You Have by Giving

To give
and to receive
are the same because
our minds are connected.

This is why it feels so
GOOD
to give someone
a hug
or a present.

If you want
people to be nice
and friendly to you,
then be nice and
friendly to
people.

Simple!

You Have Free Will

What is free will?
It means that you,
and only you,
have control over
your own mind!

Only **YOU** can
choose what types
of thoughts
you want to
believe in, and share
with others.

You are **ALWAYS**
making the choice
of how you
continue thinking.

Which path would you like to go down?
The choice is **YOURS**!

19

For example, if someone says something you do not like then it is your choice to:

- Believe what they said **OR**
- Don't believe what they said

- Reply meanly **OR**
- Reply lovingly **OR**
- Say nothing at all

- Stay and argue **OR**
- Walk away peacefully

Remember that no one can make you feel anything. It is always your choice about how to act, and how to feel. Your choices are yours.

The power of choosing is your free will!

20

Everyone is Equal

No matter what the
color of your skin is,
or where you live,
or what music you like,
or what your hobby is...

Everyone is **GOOD**
at something!

Everyone is equal.

Now, sometimes you may know someone who seems "mean"... or you see that certain people are hurting others, so you ask yourself:

'I'm a nice person, I would never hurt anyone. How could I be equal with those mean people?'

Remember that how people act comes from how they think. So if someone is acting in a hurtful way, that means they are hurting inside. They don't understand that by hurting others, they are hurting themselves. If you know someone like this and you feel comfortable, then smile at them.

They need **LOVE**, they just don't know how to ask for it.

Treat everyone equally!

22

You Will See What You Choose to Think About

Let's say that it is a rainy Saturday afternoon and you are unable to go for the bike ride you planned with your friends.

As you stare out the window watching the rain fall, you have a choice: You could think negatively and stay disappointed, **OR** you could choose to think positively and find something **FUN** to do!

When you think positively, a beautiful thing happens! It's called **POSSIBILITY**. You begin to think of other possible things you can do.

To your pleasant surprise your best bud, Tommy, calls you to go to the swim park... fun idea! Better than staring out the window.

Then you have an idea: Perhaps Tommy can stay for a sleepover?

You have a great time watching movies and hanging out, and when you wake up in the morning, the sun is shining! So you get your bike ride with your friend after all!

If you want good things to happen, then think about good things.

Let yourself be surprised by the possibilities. Choose what you want to see!

Forgiveness is the Only Thing That Heals Your Mind

Like a medicine that you take to feel better when you have a sore throat, forgiveness is the medicine that heals your mind.

How?

Because **FORGIVENESS** sets your mind **FREE** from negativity and fear.

Think of it this way...

If you judge
and condemn others
you are made a
prisoner of your
own negative
thoughts.

If you forgive,
then your mind
is **FREED**!

Forgiveness
takes practice
but it is worth it!

You deserve to have a
peaceful mind so that you
can be the BEST person
you can be ♥

To help you feel happier more often,
to help you move past tough moments,
here is a list of things you can to
to help yourself!

Everyday you can:

- not judge others

- focus on yourself and
  what makes you smile

- believe in yourself and move
  forward with your goals

When you are upset or overwhelmed you can...

❖ Stop reacting without thinking.

❖ Take some deep breaths. This is called taking a "breather."

❖ Get away from the negative situation. Go to another room and clear your head.

❖ Go play a sport or do something physical.

These choices will help you calm down.

28

When you are feeling better you can...

❖ Practice "The Switch".

❖ Forgive.

❖ Ask someone you trust for help in
thinking more positively.

❖ List the people and things you are grateful for.

We've covered a lot!
But remember, understanding
how your mind works and how powerful
your thoughts are will help you to
live a **HAPPY** life!

Parents' Guide

*"The power of decision is your one remaining freedom as
a prisoner of this world. You can decide to see it right."*
— A COURSE IN MIRACLES

CHILDREN are the world's symbol for innocence. They are imaginative, and tend to be more carefree and confident than most adults. But from a spiritual perspective, they are just like the rest of us adults. There is a part of their minds, that we can call the soul, which made the decision to come into this world in order to experience physicality. Beyond their "bundle of innocence" appearance, children have egos and it does not take a parent long to notice it.

Everyone knows that it is not always going to be sunshine and lollipops when communicating with children for they have their personalities, inherent preferences, styles and quirks which make them selfish, sensitive and irrational. As a parent or guardian, it would be helpful for you to acknowledge that not only are you training a newbie to the world, but you are living every day with an individual and very complex ego.

The ego is what is commonly referred to as the "small self" — or as I like to call it, "the cheeky lil' monkey in the corner of your mind." However you regard the ego does not matter, as long as you realize that the ego is essentially a "mis-thought," a mistake in human thinking. It is a hindrance to our peace of mind and is the source of all fear. Your child's ego is equally ready to make him or her feel like a victim of this world.

The ego sets up a world where fear runs rampant and where most people live out their lives reacting to fear. Your children will probably learn more about the ego than about the calm and spiritual part of themselves. Unfortunately, what will ensue is an identification with the fear-based part of their mind instead of the loving part.

In the following dialogue, Eckhart Tolle answers the question of a concerned parent and suggests how a recognition of the ego's thought patterns may be encouraged in children.

Questioner: They label themselves, as well. I've noticed this with my daughter, she will come home and say "I'm stupid" at this or that.

Eckhart Tolle: That's a good way to encourage her not to identify with her thoughts... If you can somehow work with them to have them realize that they are not their thoughts, so that there's a space between them and their thoughts, to observe their thoughts, and when thoughts come you can explain "it's no more than a thought" and it may not be the reality, it may not be true.

Encourage that kind of thing, so that they are able to look at the emotion that takes them over from time to time. And after the event, not during the event initially, say to them, "What was it that took you over when you started screaming yesterday? What was that?" and say, "What does it feel like?" or invent some game, so that you can make it into something that they can be aware of.

32

How many children do you know that are afraid of something, or are very sensitive? And how many children don't know how to react calmly when something negative happens? These are examples of a victim mentality, wherein children believe they are susceptible to external events and opinions.

Your child's identification with the ego will be sustained through judgment and their comparison of themselves to others. "This day sucks"; "I'm embarrassed"; "Ugh, I don't want to do that"; "They can, but I *can't* do that!" are the types of judgments which will hinder your child's potential for positive mental development and inevitably lower their self-esteem. But if your child learns that by judging themselves and others, they are ultimately making life much harder for themselves, they may decide to relinquish their judgments in favour of a peaceful state of mind. This is a choice that they deserve to know exists, because they are going to feel the consequences of their thinking very strongly and on a daily basis.

This book is based on the cognitive principles presented in the metaphysical masterpiece *A Course in Miracles* (ACIM). For those who are unfamiliar with the text of ACIM, it presents an analysis of how the ego (the false self) works, how Spirit (our reality) works, and the distinctions between the two. There is a corresponding Workbook consisting of 365 daily lessons which are focused on undoing the ego, so the student can experience and identify with the underlying core of what they really are: love.

Love and Spirit are synonyms according to ACIM. The teaching urges us not to attack the ego, nor make friends with it, but simply to disidentify from the ego through the process of true forgiveness. As ACIM states: *"…you cannot escape from the ego by humbling it or controlling it or punishing it."* Thus, we cannot attack the ego because that would be making it real in the mind. Our judgments determine what is real for us, dictating our belief systems and thus guiding how we function in the world.

Throughout its text, ACIM presents "laws of the mind" that govern how the mind properly functions. These laws are simple and their truth becomes evident through the students' application of the lesson. ACIM itself is meant for adults. This book aims at presenting to children the simple principles of how their thoughts and ideas work, and how they can use them positively. They will also learn how to manage ego upsets and gain coping mechanisms to help them relax more easily.

The mind is malleable, and children can be taught a loving and healthy mindset with less resistance than adults. Children are sponges for information, so if you begin offering the laws of the mind as soon as you can they will hear you, watch your demonstration, and absorb that knowledge. You will be helping them become healthy-minded, calm and compassionate adults! As adults we wish we could be by the side of our young loved ones at every moment so we could guide them and protect them. My dear hope for this book is that the knowledge contained within it will be your child's lifelong companion, guiding them lovingly along their path.

"Peace of mind is clearly an internal matter. It must begin with your own thoughts, and then extend outward. It is from your peace of mind that a peaceful perception of the world arises." — A COURSE IN MIRACLES

Five Tips for Speaking
Effectively With Your Child

Tip 1

Clear your mental space. Release any mental preoccupations like "what to make for dinner?" and such. Some parents may feel inconvenienced by their child's emotional outbursts, viewing them as unnecessary interruptions of the day's events. Always be aware that your child can pick up on your true feelings through your tone, behaviour and posture, so you want to be mindful of the attitude you are presenting. Relax with the commitment to take a few minutes to interact fully with your children, and be fully present.

Approach your child with a calm tone of patience and love. Remain non-accusatory and feel out the situation of what is bothering them. This is easily accomplished by looking at them lovingly right in their eyes.

When people feel threatened or fearful, they naturally shut down, resorting to silence or even deception. For children, telling lies or being silent can easily turn into habits of avoidance. If your children feel that they are not being heard or that you don't trust them, then they will want to avoid talking about the truth. Set a healthy tone by encouraging loving, meaningful conversation.

Tip 2

Clear your physical space. When you are speaking seriously with your child, take care that you are not in an area where there are many distractions. You can leave your phone and any other attention-getting devices out of the room, teaching your child how to be fully present when speaking with others. As you well know, meltdowns sometimes occur in public spaces, so follow your heart and gauge the level of urgency from your child's perspective. See if it is appropriate to engage with your child in helpful conversation where you are, or whether you need to find some space outside or in another room. Or you may have to postpone a talk until you can get home. Ask your children to be honest, and let them tell you when or where they want to talk about it. Show them that you trust their opinions and decisions.

Tip 3

Get to your children's level. Show them that problems are solved with peaceful communication and understanding from both sides. Ensure that your children know that you are there for them, and encourage them to use words to describe how they're feeling, instead of just grunting or groaning. If a child is a bit younger, he or she may not know the words to use, so use your intuition and observe their body language. As a parent, you know your children, so if you put in the effort you will easily come to understand how they're feeling and what they're saying.

You are their safe place. In order to have your child grow into an adult with a healthy voice, you have to let them know that their voice deserves to be heard. You also have an excellent opportunity to feel out any negativity that may be occurring in their life when you're not around, like their experiences at school, extracurricular activities or even at friend's homes.

Tip 4

Do not punish your children. Instead, help them to understand. People do better when they understand *why* they should or shouldn't do something. Punishment is a fear-based motivation and does nothing but reinforce your child's ego. As *A Course in Miracles* suggests, *"Learning through rewards is more effective than learning through pain, because pain is an ego illusion, and can never induce more than a temporary effect."* In this light, an effective "reward" can be anything that is loving, which includes peaceful communication, education, and the opportunity to let kids learn from their mistakes without a slap on the wrist. For example, let's reflect on 'grounding' your child as a punishment. This is incredibly isolating for a young person who's already aggravated; it adds a sense of alienation to his negative thinking. His angry state of mind which led him to act out in the first place is now compounded by feeling misunderstood, and can add to self-hatred.

We never know why children do some of the things they decide to do, but that's just as true for adults. The aim is to listen to your children and find the reasons for their actions. If they do act out, they will feel guilty for they know deep down that whatever they did wasn't cool. They don't need you or anyone else to reinforce that guilt. But you can help them to work throught guilt and anger in order to get them to a more loving place in their minds. **As their loving guardian, the power is in your hands to reinforce love or fear.**

Tip 5

Believe in the good in your children. Believe that they can overcome whatever issues they are facing. Teach them about the strength that exists inside of them by *showing* them that strength. For your minds are connected, and your belief in them will amplify their belief in themselves. Tell them as much, let them know they have a fan, a supporter and a believer by their side.

This work is a collaboration. May this knowledge be helpful for you, your growing children and the relationships you have with them.

Acknowledgments

I would like to acknowledge my dear fiancé, Eric Visser, for providing me with the opportunity to focus on and fully pursue this heartfelt project. Thank you for seeing how strongly I wanted to write this book. I know that you want to see this book in the hands of every child too. I am so grateful for you. I love you.

I would also like to acknowledge my father, David Williams, for illustrating the book. Your imagination and creativity has brought my dream to life! It has been so much fun working with you. Thank you for your commitment. I love you.

And finally I would like to acknowledge D. Patrick Miller of Fearless Books. Thank you dearly for your support in helping me to complete this project. I'm beyond thrilled that this book came to be through your helpful guidance!